FeelLinks®

A feeling journal for children

Marcelle Waldman

Manufactured in China
FeelLinks, Inc.
Issaquah, WA 98027
myfeellinks.com

FeelLinks Goals

FeelLinks journal and dolls were intentionally created as a hands-on resource supporting children in building emotional intelligence. Children will become more comfortable with recognizing, labeling, expressing, and managing their own feelings and the feelings of others.

- To provide children a tangible tool to express their feelings and emotions through drawing, writing*, communicating*, and role-playing.

- To develop an understanding that it is common for everyone to experience positive and uncomfortable feelings.

- To foster an understanding that feelings are valid and important and meant to be expressed.

- To build a greater emotional vocabulary.

- To support growth in self-awareness skills by understanding and taking personal responsibility for their emotions.

- To nurture positive relationship skills with themselves and others, serving them throughout life.

*A little note on writing: Writing is a developmental skill. Some young children may or may not want to take a risk in putting down words in their journal. Writing has meaning in a variety of forms. Anything from a scribble, random letters, and beginning sounds, to phonetically spelled or correctly spelled words. In no way should this be an assessment of your child's writing skills. You may have your child dictate what they would like the words to say, then you write for them. The "writing" lines should be utilized in the way that best fits your child.

*A little note on communication: *FeelLinks* journal and dolls are tools that can be used with both verbal and non-verbal communications.

Emotional Intelligence

Emotional intelligence is the ability to identify, understand, and manage your own emotions and the emotions of others. People with high emotional intelligence demonstrate an understanding of what they are feeling, what their emotions mean, and how their emotions impact others.

Research shows that those with high emotional intelligence are typically more successful in life — with higher satisfaction at school and work, increased academic achievement, quality relationships and greater empathy. High emotional intelligence is key to knowing one's self, relating to others, sensing the emotional needs of others, and achieving personal goals.

FeelLinks was created with the knowledge that emotional intelligence can be taught, learned and further developed with the support of adult coaching and modeling.

Fostering emotional intelligence means building skills in knowing and managing your emotions, motivating yourself, recognizing and understanding other people's emotions, and managing relationships.

These five areas are broken down into four parts: self-awareness, social-awareness, self-management, and relationship skills.

SELF-AWARENESS:

» **accurate self-assessment**

» **awareness of your emotional state**

» **intrinsic motivation**

» **perseverance**

» **self-confidence**

SOCIAL AWARENESS:

» **empathy**

» **getting along with others**

» **reading other's expression, voice, and tone**

» **sensing other's feelings**

RELATIONSHIP MANAGEMENT:

- » building bonds
- » clearly expressing ideas
- » conflict management
- » influencing inspiration
- » leadership
- » managing interactions successfully
- » teamwork and collaboration

SELF-MANAGEMENT

- » adaptability
- » emotional self-control/ regulation
- » flexibility/handling change
- » optimism/growth mindset
- » pursuing goals

Adapted from "Emotional Intelligence" by Daniel Goleman

Guide to using FeelLinks

FeelLinks journal and dolls were created to be used in a variety of ways, depending on what is best for your child and you. Using *FeelLinks* journal to express feelings daily, will be a beneficial practice for your child. Whichever way you choose to utilize *FeelLinks*, know that you are helping your child understand and take personal responsibility for their feelings and emotions. *FeelLinks* journal and dolls are designed to encourage your child to express their feelings through communication, role-play, drawing, and writing, all while connecting with you. With adult modeling, coaching, and continued practice, children will learn that they can safely express and manage their feelings in a healthy manner.

Remember, it is important that children understand all types of feelings, both positive and uncomfortable. Please be sure to also use *FeelLinks* when your child is having positive feelings and responses; this is an important part of the process in building emotional intelligence and positive relationships with others.

Take as many opportunities as possible to point out the positive and uncomfortable feelings you notice your child experiencing. Praise your child when they express emotions in appropriate ways. The more we teach children that the feelings they are experiencing are common to us all, the better they will be at proactively managing their feelings.

FeelLinks Dolls

FeelLinks dolls represent eight core feelings which are intended to be built upon with 'words to grow on', which are found in the *FeelLinks* journal. When children expand their emotional vocabulary, and more specifically label their feelings, adults are better able to support their needs.

Each doll's facial expression and coordinating feeling color will help your child relate their feelings with the doll's feelings. *FeelLinks* dolls are a comfortable, cuddly, and safe way to help your child express all of their feelings! Children can communicate verbally and non-verbally with their *FeelLinks* dolls. Children may relate to multiple dolls when experiencing a mix of emotions.

How to Use FeelLinks Dolls

FeelLinks dolls are intended to be a tool for calming, expressing, and communicating.

Calming techniques could include: cuddling, squeezing, tossing, or placing on the child's belly and taking deep breaths together. Dolls are also great for role-playing, talking, laughing, or crying together.

Dolls as communication tools could include: showing you which doll(s) represents their current or past feelings, naming doll's feelings, connecting doll's feelings to their own feelings, sharing aloud how they are feeling either individually or in a group setting.

FeelLinks dolls can be used at any time and in any way that fits your individual child's needs.

FeelLinks Head, Heart, and Belly Touchpoints

Head

Heart

Belly

All feelings, whether positive or uncomfortable, are felt throughout our body. It is crucial to question, point out and discuss how your child's head, heart, and belly feel during and after emotional responses.

HAPPY

PROUD

SAD

EMBARRASSED

CALM

EXCITED

ANGRY

SCARED

FeelLinks Journal Benefits

FeelLinks journal empowers children to reflect and respond to their feelings; encouraging growth in identifying, understanding, and managing their emotions.

Journaling is a process in self-awareness, reflection, social growth, and problem-solving, in a non-judgmental place. Journaling has many wonderful benefits for your child, including:

- Processing and expressing feelings through drawing and/or writing.
- Encouraging communication with a trusted adult.
- Building broader emotional vocabulary through the words to grow on.
- Supporting emotional and physical health by reducing stress and anxiety through expressing feelings instead of holding them inside.
- Building creativity and strengthening fine motor skills through drawing and writing.
- Practicing expressive writing, spelling, vocabulary, sentence structure, and handwriting skills.

Using FeelLinks Journal

Write the date.

I am feeling…This is an opportunity for reflection. Child will label their feelings by circling the *FeelLinks* doll(s) that represents how they are feeling.
- » Help your child recall how their head, heart, and belly felt during their emotional response.

Child will draw pictures that might include:
- » What happened?
- » How did they/others respond?
- » How did they express their feelings?
- » How did they manage/regulate their feelings?
- » What problem-solving strategies did they use?

Add words. This is an option your child may choose.
- » Label pictures.
- » Write about feelings and experiences.
- » Dictate to an adult.

Now I am feeling…
- » Child will color in *FeelLinks* doll(s) that represents how they are feeling after journaling. Blank dolls can be used for labeling feelings more specifically.

As your child grows more comfortable and confident in using their *FeelLinks* journal, they may begin to journal without support. This is fantastic!

Child will circle *FeelLinks* doll(s) that shows how they are feeling.

A space for your child to draw anything related to their feelings, emotional response, problem-solving strategies, and more.

Writing the date can help with noticing any trends in your child's feelings.

Space for your child to write or an adult to listen to the child's words and dictate in *FeelLinks* journal.

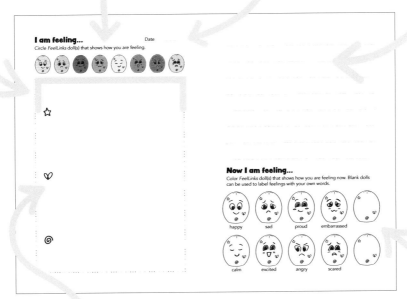

A reminder for your child to think about and draw what their head, heart, and belly feel like during and after their emotional response.

Child will color in *FeelLinks* doll(s) that shows how they are feeling after journaling. Blank dolls can be used for labeling feelings more specifically.

Strengthening Emotional Intelligence

Emotions are an opportunity to connect with your child. Steps you can take to connect and encourage development in emotional intelligence include:

FIND YOUR CALM. This can be difficult when emotions are heightened, but it's certainly one of the best tools in your toolbox.

GET ON YOUR CHILD'S LEVEL. Move gently, use a calm voice, get down on your child's level, and make eye contact, showing them an important message of safety, trust, and care.

ASSURANCE. *"I am here for you."* You might also offer a gentle hand on their shoulder or a hug, if desired.

LISTEN. Listen to your child's perspective as they recognize their feelings. Try staying quiet as they open up. Support them if they are in need of coaching.

EXPRESS. Let your child continue to express their feelings. Try saying, *"It is okay that you are feeling (frustrated), we all get (frustrated)."* *FeelLinks* dolls can support this step. If your child exhibits behaviors that are not acceptable, be sure to calmly set limits. All feelings are okay, but not all behaviors are okay.

VALIDATE. EMPATHIZE. Let your child know that you understand what they are expressing and show empathy. *"I can see how hard that was for you."*

LABEL. Labeling feelings helps us better support the child. Help your child with labeling their feeling(s). They will need support in learning new vocabulary, understanding sensations in their head, heart and belly, tone of voice, and facial expressions, in order to develop skills in labeling. *FeelLinks* supports this step.

CO-REGULATE. REGULATE. Continue supporting your child in regulating their feelings and finding their preferred strategies for calming. Children will differ in duration getting back to calm after heightened emotions. *Discuss calming strategies outside of heightened emotional moments. *FeelLinks* journal and dolls are great support tools for regulation.

REFLECT. RESPOND. It's typically best to reflect when emotions are calm. Access *FeelLinks* journal for your child to reflect and respond to their feelings.

PROBLEM SOLVE. Sometimes you need to problem solve with your child 'in the moment'. If this is the case, you need to be firm, clear, set boundaries, limit your verbal communication, and give alternatives. Other times, problem-solving occurs when your child is calm. This helps your child learn, boosts self-confidence, and increases their ability to make better choices at another time. *"What could you do instead?"* *"How can I help you next time?"* *"Is there another way to think about it?"*

MOVE ON. Read, bake, play catch, listen to music, sing, dance, tell jokes, watch a show – do something to continue connecting while moving forward.

*These steps may not all happen in one interaction. This will depend on the child and the situation. Patience is key.

FIND YOUR CALM AND CONNECT

Child exhibits emotional response to feelings (positive or uncomfortable).

PERMISSION AND ASSURANCE

Get on your child's level. Let them know it's okay to feel their feelings. Assure them that you are there for them. "I am here for you. I am listening."

LISTEN

Listen to child's perspective. Try remaining quiet, unless they need coaching in processing their feelings.

Child can access FeelLinks dolls and choose the doll(s) that corresponds to their feeling(s).

EXPRESS

Child continues to express feelings appropriately. If not, calmly set limits and give alternatives. *FeelLinks* dolls can assist with expression.

VALIDATE AND EMPATHIZE

Rephrase what child is expressing. Show empathy by letting them know you hear what they are expressing and you understand what they are experiencing.

LABEL

After you have fully listened, support child in developing and utilizing vocabulary for labeling their feelings. *FeelLinks* Dolls and Journal support these skills.

REGULATE

Coach child in regulating emotional response back to calm. Discuss affects in their bodies: head, heart, and belly. Use *FeelLinks* dolls to assist.

REFLECT AND RESPOND

When emotions are calm, access *FeelLinks* journal for child to reflect and respond to their feelings.

PROBLEM SOLVE

Teach problem solving strategies and appropriate behavioral responses: "What could you do instead?" "How can I help you?" Child can add these to their journal.

"When little people are overwhelmed by big emotions, it's our job to share our calm, not join their chaos." - L.R. Knost

Essential Support

Supporting a child's use of *FeelLinks* journal and dolls is essential and intended to nurture a child's emotional growth.

Adults will want to begin by modeling the use of *FeelLinks* journal and dolls:

- How do you recognize, label, express, and regulate your feelings?
- How do you verbally and non-verbally communicate and relate to *FeelLinks* dolls?
- How do you record your feelings and problem-solving strategies in *FeelLinks* journal?

Role-playing, drawing, writing, and communicating your feelings help children understand that feelings are a common experience.

FeelLinks Grows with Your Child

FeelLinks has eight core feelings with more 'words to grow on'. The emotional vocabulary is meant to grow with your child. Take time to introduce more complex feeling words. The more words children have to express their emotions, the better we are able to support them.

As your child grows comfortable with using their *FeelLinks* journal, they may enjoy picking it up on their own time and sharing it with you.

FeelLinks Grows with You

An incredible gift you can provide your child is to continue growing and working on your emotional intelligence. You will be able to model and teach your child how to understand, label, express, and regulate their feelings better, if you take time to reflect on how you handle your feelings.

When emotions are high, find your calm. Know your triggers. These are often past experiences in your emotional memory bank, or caused by your values being violated.

Use calming strategies that work best for you, such as: Self-talk - choose a phrase and repeat it to yourself. Best-self - imagine your 'best-self' and respond that way. Deep breaths - slow, deep breaths will actually change the chemicals in your body and reduce stress hormones. Self-care - the more you practice self-care, the more relaxed you will be to calmly respond.

Establishing FeelLinks Journal Guidelines with Your Child

1. **Who is allowed to draw/write in your *FeelLinks* journal?**

   Will your child be the only one to write/draw in their journal or will an adult also be permitted to use the journal for modeling purposes?

2. **Who is allowed to see your *FeelLinks* journal?**

   Trust is important when writing in a journal. Decide who is permitted to see what is recorded inside.

3. **Your *FeelLinks* journal is space to draw/write anything about your feelings.**

   What you choose to put inside your journal should not be changed or edited by anyone else.

This journal belongs to

....

....

We feel emotions in our whole body.

When you are feeling different emotions, where do you feel them? You can ask yourself...

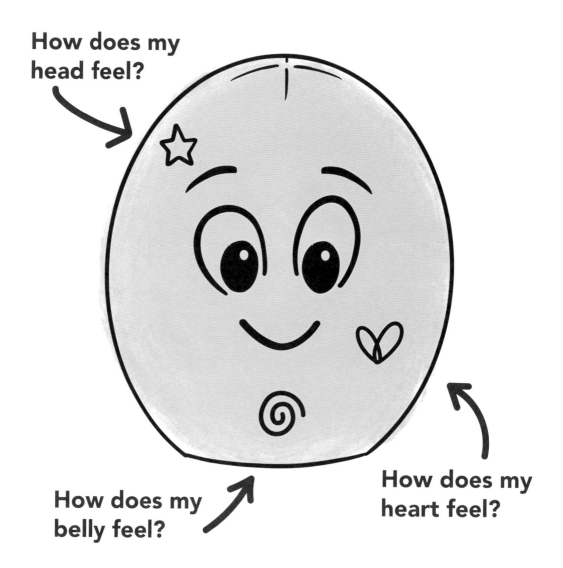

How does my head feel?

How does my belly feel?

How does my heart feel?

Ways to help me calm my body and mind.

HUG SOMEONE

READ A BOOK

DO A PUZZLE

CUDDLE OR SQUEEZE FeelLinks DOLL

HAVE SOME ALONE TIME

BUILD SOMETHING

PAINT

GET A DRINK OF WATER

COUNT

DRAW OR COLOR

LISTEN TO CALM MUSIC

DO 10 JUMPING JACKS

DEEP BREATHS – PLACE FeelLinks DOLL ON YOUR BELLY AND BREATHE TOGETHER

GO OUTDOORS

Deep Breathing Exercises

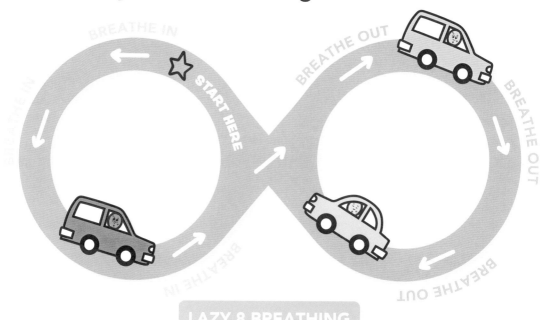

LAZY 8 BREATHING

Trace the Lazy 8 racetrack with your finger. Starting at the star, take a deep breath in. As you cross over to the other side of the Lazy 8 racetrack, slowly let your breath out. Continue breathing until you have a calm body and mind.

STAR BREATHING

Trace the star with your finger. Starting at the dot, take a deep breath in, hold, then slowly breathe out. Be sure to hold your breath for a few seconds at each point. Follow your way around the star. Continue breathing until you have a calm body and mind.

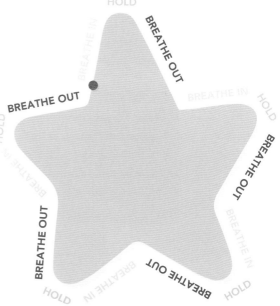

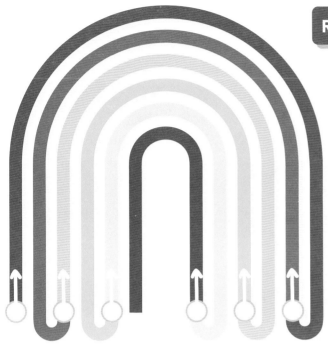

RAINBOW BREATHING

Trace the rainbow with your finger. Starting at the dot on the color red, follow the arrow over the arch, take a long deep breath in. Pause at the end of the red arch. While tracing the color orange, slowly breathe out. Be sure to take it nice and slow as you move through the rest of the colors of the rainbow. Continue breathing until you have a calm body and mind.

BOX BREATHING

Trace the box with your finger. Starting at the dot, take a slow, deep breath in for 4 seconds. Pause, gently holding your breath for 4 seconds. Slowly breathe out for 4 seconds. Continue breathing in for 4, holding for 4, and out for 4, until you have a calm body and mind.

A mix of emotions.

We feel many shades of emotions, one at a time or many at once.

Fun Pages

About me

Age:

My birthday:

Favorite place:

Favorite color:

City:

I am good at:

Hobbies:

Favorite animal:

Favorite book:

School:

Favorite food:

Many feeling faces of me

Draw your face expressing each feeling.

Happy

Sad

Proud

Embarrassed

Calm

Excited

Angry

Scared

My family

My school

My community

This is how I feel about...

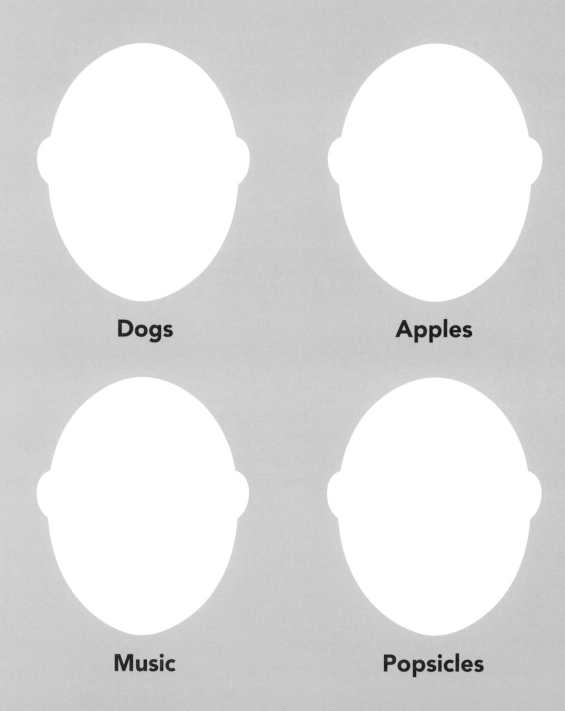

Dogs

Apples

Music

Popsicles

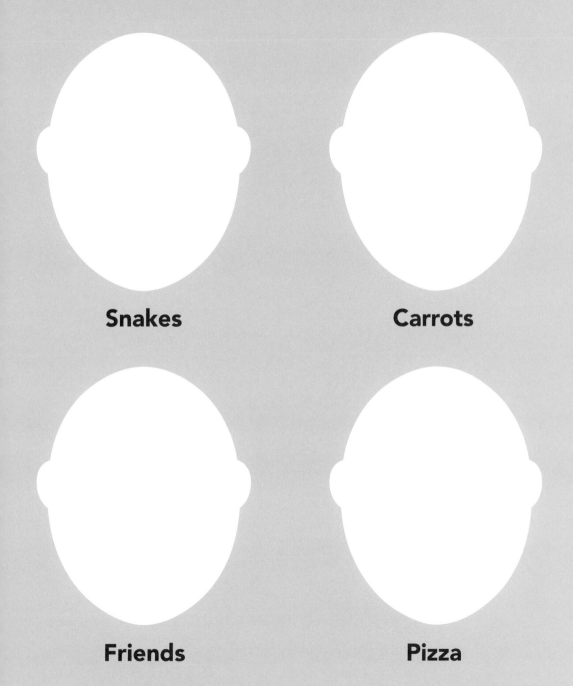

Snakes

Carrots

Friends

Pizza

Weather gives me feelings

Our feelings are a lot like the weather, they are always changing. Color *FeelLinks* dolls to show what feelings the weather gives you.

Windy

| happy | sad | proud | embarrassed | calm | excited | angry | scared |

Lightning

| happy | sad | proud | embarrassed | calm | excited | angry | scared |

Snowy

| happy | sad | proud | embarrassed | calm | excited | angry | scared |

Rainy

| happy | sad | proud | embarrassed | calm | excited | angry | scared |

Partly Cloudy

| happy | sad | proud | embarrassed | calm | excited | angry | scared |

Cloudy

| happy | sad | proud | embarrassed | calm | excited | angry | scared |

Sunny

| happy | sad | proud | embarrassed | calm | excited | angry | scared |

I feel grateful

We feel grateful for things big and small. What are you grateful for?

Gratitude Scavenger Hunt

I can hunt for things I am grateful for...

☐ Something that makes me feel happy.

☐ Something that I love doing on my own.

☐ Something that is my favorite color.

☐ Something that I love doing with a family member.

☐ A food I love to eat.

☐ A favorite book to read.

☐ Something that makes me laugh.

☐ Something I love.

Parts of Your Brain

- decision making
- imagination
- learning
- problem solving
- reasoning
- speaking
- thoughts

PREFRONTAL CORTEX
(front of your brain)

**THE WISE LEADER
THINKING BRAIN**

**FEELING
BRAIN**

LIMBIC SYSTEM
(middle of your brain)

AMYGDALA
The guard dog
- behavior
- emotions
- motivation
- protection

**THE REPTILE
INSTINCTUAL
BRAIN**

HIPPOCAMPUS
The librarian
- memories
- stores learning

BRAINSTEM
(bottom of your brain)

Automatic functions
- blinking
- breathing
- heart beating
- swallowing
- sweating

Survival reactions
- fight
- flight
- freeze
- collapse

My brain is awesome!

Draw the things in your brain.

My Doodles

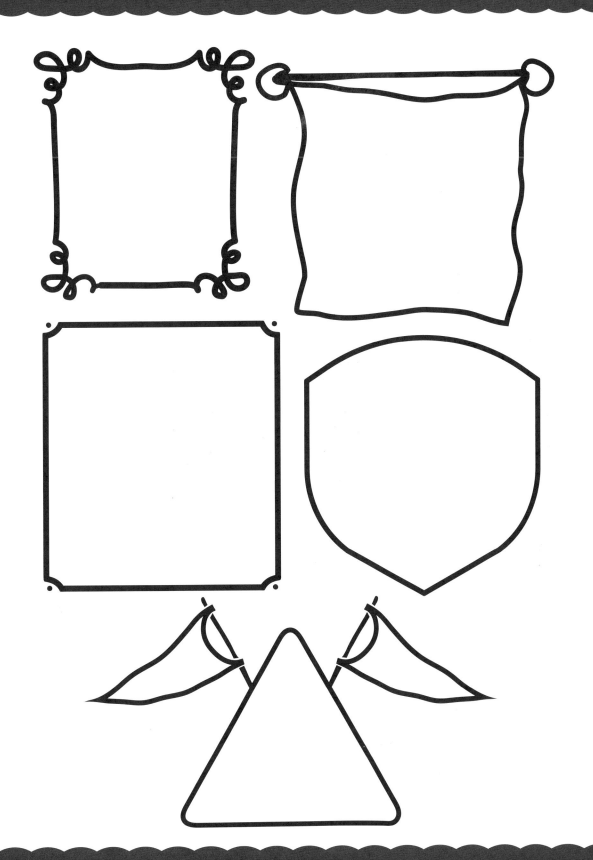

Happy

Feeling great pleasure or joy.

Words to grow on:

Cheerful
Bright and pleasant.

Fortunate
Having good luck.

Fulfilled
Happy and satisfied about life.

Glad
Experiencing pleasure, joy or delight.

Glowing
So happy and satisfied that you feel like you are glowing.

Grateful
The quality of feeling thankful.

Joyful
Full of joy, very happy.

Merry
Smiling and cheerful.

Thankful
Feeling or showing of appreciation.

I felt happy when...

Draw or write about a time when you felt happy.

Other things that make me feel happy.

Draw or write about what else makes you feel happy.

Sad

Filled with grief or unhappiness.

Words to grow on:

Disappointed
Upset over something that is not like you thought it would be.

Gloomy
Everything feels darker than usual; causing feelings of sadness.

Grief
Deep sadness; especially for the loss of someone or something.

Grumpy
In a bad, sad mood.

Heartbroken
Extremely sad, like your heart is breaking into pieces.

Helpless
Feeling there is no one to help you.

Hurt
Unhappiness or sadness caused by someone's words or actions.

Lonely
Being alone and feeling sad about it.

Mopey
Droopy and sad.

Unhappy
Not cheerful.

Upset
Unhappy like you could cry.

I felt sad when...

Draw or write about a time when you felt sad.

Other things that make me feel sad.

Draw or write about what else makes you feel sad.

Proud

Displaying excessive self-esteem and self-respect.

Words to grow on:

Brave
Feeling or displaying no fear; courageous.

Confident
Self-assured in your own powers and abilities.

Courageous
Not letting fear hold you back. Doing what is right.

Delighted
Extremely happy.

Fulfilled
Feeling that your abilities and talents are fully being used.

I feel proud when...

Draw or write about a time when you felt **proud**.

Other things that make me feel proud.

Draw or write about what else makes you feel proud.

Embarrassed

Feeling self-consciously confused or distressed.

Words to grow on:

Ashamed

Feeling shame or guilt.

Awkward

Causing embarrassment. Lacking in skill.

Confused

Unable to understand or think clearly.

Flustered

Nervous confusion.

Self-conscious

Being aware of yourself and questioning how you appear to others.

Shy

Not feeling comfortable around others; not wanting or being able to call attention to yourself.

Uncomfortable

Uneasy feeling in your body.

I feel embarrassed when...

Draw or write about a time when you felt embarrassed.

Other things that make me feel embarrassed.

Draw or write about what else makes you feel embarrassed.

Calm

Free from excitement or disturbance.

Words to grow on:

Content

Satisfied.

Fulfilled

Having everything you need.

Peaceful

Enjoying peace and quiet.

Relaxed

Not worried or tense.

Relieved

Without fear or worry.

Restful

Relax, sleep or without activity.

Satisfied

Happy with what you have; needing nothing else.

Tranquil

Without noise or excitement.

I feel calm when...

Draw or write about a time when you felt calm.

Other things that make me feel calm.

Draw or write about what else makes you feel calm.

Excited

Having or showing a strong energized feeling.

Words to grow on:

Eager

Having or showing an impatient or enthusiastic interest or desire.

Ecstatic

Overwhelming, extreme pleasurable emotion.

Enthusiastic

Liking something a lot and being very interested in it.

Thrilled

Experiencing a sudden, strong feeling of excitement.

I feel excited when...

Draw or write about a time when you felt **excited**.

Other things that make me feel excited.

Draw or write about what else makes you feel **excited**.

Angry

Strongly feeling great annoyance, pain, trouble or displeasure.

Words to grow on:

Annoyed
Being made angry by someone or something.

Cranky
Being easily angered.

Envious
Resentful, usually because you want something that someone else has.

Frustrated
Feeling you did not get what you want or need.

Fuming
So angry, like steam is coming out of your ears.

Furious
Extremely angry.

Grumpy
In a bad mood.

Irritated
Feeling displeasured or stirred to anger.

Jealous
Feeling envy of what someone else has or can do. Resentful.

Mad
Very displeased.

Overwhelmed
Overcome with emotion.

Stressed
Feeling mental or emotional strain or tension.

Upset
Worried, angered or unhappy.

I feel angry when...

Draw or write about a time when you felt angry.

Other things that make me feel angry.

Draw or write about what else makes you feel **angry**.

Scared

Being in a state of fear, fright or panic.

Words to grow on:

Afraid

Filled with concern or fear.

Anxious

Worried something is going to happen that will be scary for you.

Concerned

Worried or anxious about a person or thing.

Fearful

Full of fear or worry about danger.

Jittery

Jumpy with nerves.

Nervous

Edgy, worried and jumpy.

Panicked

Out of control with fear.

Shocked

Stunned, dazed and upset.

Stressed

Worried and frazzled.

Tense

Your muscles have tensed up, your jaw is clenched, and you are worried.

Terrified

Scared stiff.

Worried

Concerned and anxious about something.

I feel scared when...

Draw or write about a time when you felt scared.

Other things that make me feel scared.

Draw or write about what else makes you feel scared.

Journal

Here are my favorite ways to calm my body and mind

I am feeling...

Circle *FeelLinks* doll(s) that shows how you are feeling.

....

....

....

....

....

....

....

Now I am feeling...

Color *FeelLinks* doll(s) that shows how you are feeling now. Blank dolls can be used to label feelings with your own words.

| happy | sad | proud | embarrassed | |
| calm | excited | angry | scared | |

I am feeling...

Date............................

Circle *FeelLinks* doll(s) that shows how you are feeling.

....

....

....

....

....

....

....

Now I am feeling...

Color *FeelLinks* doll(s) that shows how you are feeling now. Blank dolls can be used to label feelings with your own words.

| happy | sad | proud | embarrassed | |
| calm | excited | angry | scared | |

I am feeling...

Circle *FeelLinks* doll(s) that shows how you are feeling.

....

....

....

....

....

....

....

Now I am feeling...

Color *FeelLinks* doll(s) that shows how you are feeling now. Blank dolls can be used to label feelings with your own words.

| happy | sad | proud | embarrassed | |
| calm | excited | angry | scared | |

I am feeling...

Date ....

Circle *FeelLinks* doll(s) that shows how you are feeling.

....

....

....

....

....

....

....

Now I am feeling...

Color *FeelLinks* doll(s) that shows how you are feeling now. Blank dolls can be used to label feelings with your own words.

happy   sad   proud   embarrassed

calm   excited   angry   scared

I am feeling...

Circle *FeelLinks* doll(s) that shows how you are feeling.

....

....

....

....

....

....

Now I am feeling...

Color *FeelLinks* doll(s) that shows how you are feeling now. Blank dolls can be used to label feelings with your own words.

happy   sad   proud   embarrassed

calm   excited   angry   scared

I am feeling...

Circle *FeelLinks* doll(s) that shows how you are feeling.

....

....

....

....

....

....

....

Now I am feeling...

Color *FeelLinks* doll(s) that shows how you are feeling now. Blank dolls can be used to label feelings with your own words.

happy   sad   proud   embarrassed

calm   excited   angry   scared

I am feeling...

Date ....

Circle *FeelLinks* doll(s) that shows how you are feeling.

....

....

....

....

....

....

....

....

Now I am feeling...

Color *FeelLinks* doll(s) that shows how you are feeling now. Blank dolls can be used to label feelings with your own words.

happy   sad   proud   embarrassed

calm   excited   angry   scared

I am feeling...

Circle *FeelLinks* doll(s) that shows how you are feeling.

....

....

....

....

....

....

....

Now I am feeling...

Color *FeelLinks* doll(s) that shows how you are feeling now. Blank dolls can be used to label feelings with your own words.

happy   sad   proud   embarrassed

calm   excited   angry   scared

I am feeling...

Circle *FeelLinks* doll(s) that shows how you are feeling.

....

....

....

....

....

....

....

Now I am feeling...

Color *FeelLinks* doll(s) that shows how you are feeling now. Blank dolls can be used to label feelings with your own words.

happy   sad   proud   embarrassed

calm   excited   angry   scared

I am feeling...

Circle *FeelLinks* doll(s) that shows how you are feeling.

....

....

....

....

....

....

Now I am feeling...

Color *FeelLinks* doll(s) that shows how you are feeling now. Blank dolls can be used to label feelings with your own words.

happy   sad   proud   embarrassed

calm   excited   angry   scared

I am feeling...

Date ....

Circle *FeelLinks* doll(s) that shows how you are feeling.

....

....

....

....

....

....

....

Now I am feeling...

Color *FeelLinks* doll(s) that shows how you are feeling now. Blank dolls can be used to label feelings with your own words.

happy   sad   proud   embarrassed

calm   excited   angry   scared

I am feeling...

Circle *FeelLinks* doll(s) that shows how you are feeling.

....

....

....

....

....

....

....

Now I am feeling...

Color *FeelLinks* doll(s) that shows how you are feeling now. Blank dolls can be used to label feelings with your own words.

happy   sad   proud   embarrassed

calm   excited   angry   scared

I am feeling...

Circle *FeelLinks* doll(s) that shows how you are feeling.

....

....

....

....

....

....

....

Now I am feeling...

Color *FeelLinks* doll(s) that shows how you are feeling now. Blank dolls can be used to label feelings with your own words.

| happy | sad | proud | embarrassed | |
| calm | excited | angry | scared | |

I am feeling...

Date ....

Circle *FeelLinks* doll(s) that shows how you are feeling.

....

....

....

....

....

....

....

Now I am feeling...

Color *FeelLinks* doll(s) that shows how you are feeling now. Blank dolls can be used to label feelings with your own words.

happy   sad   proud   embarrassed

calm   excited   angry   scared

I am feeling...

Circle *FeelLinks* doll(s) that shows how you are feeling.

....

....

....

....

....

....

....

Now I am feeling...

Color *FeelLinks* doll(s) that shows how you are feeling now. Blank dolls can be used to label feelings with your own words.

happy   sad   proud   embarrassed

calm   excited   angry   scared

I am feeling...

Circle *FeelLinks* doll(s) that shows how you are feeling.

....

....

....

....

....

....

....

Now I am feeling...

Color *FeelLinks* doll(s) that shows how you are feeling now. Blank dolls can be used to label feelings with your own words.

| happy | sad | proud | embarrassed | |
| calm | excited | angry | scared | |

I am feeling...

Circle *FeelLinks* doll(s) that shows how you are feeling.

....

....

....

....

....

....

Now I am feeling...

Color *FeelLinks* doll(s) that shows how you are feeling now. Blank dolls can be used to label feelings with your own words.

| happy | sad | proud | embarrassed | |
| calm | excited | angry | scared | |

I am feeling...

Date ....

Circle *FeelLinks* doll(s) that shows how you are feeling.

....

....

....

....

....

....

....

Now I am feeling...

Color *FeelLinks* doll(s) that shows how you are feeling now. Blank dolls can be used to label feelings with your own words.

happy   sad   proud   embarrassed

calm   excited   angry   scared

I am feeling...

Date ....

Circle *FeelLinks* doll(s) that shows how you are feeling.

....

....

....

....

....

....

....

Now I am feeling...

Color *FeelLinks* doll(s) that shows how you are feeling now. Blank dolls can be used to label feelings with your own words.

| happy | sad | proud | embarrassed | |
| calm | excited | angry | scared | |

I am feeling...

Circle *FeelLinks* doll(s) that shows how you are feeling.

Now I am feeling...

Color *FeelLinks* doll(s) that shows how you are feeling now. Blank dolls can be used to label feelings with your own words.

happy   sad   proud   embarrassed

calm   excited   angry   scared

I am feeling...

Date ....

Circle *FeelLinks* doll(s) that shows how you are feeling.

....

....

....

....

....

....

....

Now I am feeling...

Color *FeelLinks* doll(s) that shows how you are feeling now. Blank dolls can be used to label feelings with your own words.

happy   sad   proud   embarrassed

calm   excited   angry   scared

I am feeling...

Circle *FeelLinks* doll(s) that shows how you are feeling.

....

....

....

....

....

....

....

Now I am feeling...

Color *FeelLinks* doll(s) that shows how you are feeling now. Blank dolls can be used to label feelings with your own words.

| happy | sad | proud | embarrassed | |
| calm | excited | angry | scared | |

I am feeling...

Date ....

Circle *FeelLinks* doll(s) that shows how you are feeling.

....

....

....

....

....

....

....

Now I am feeling...

Color *FeelLinks* doll(s) that shows how you are feeling now. Blank dolls can be used to label feelings with your own words.

happy   sad   proud   embarrassed

calm   excited   angry   scared

I am feeling...

Circle *FeelLinks* doll(s) that shows how you are feeling.

....

....

....

....

....

....

....

Now I am feeling...

Color *FeelLinks* doll(s) that shows how you are feeling now. Blank dolls can be used to label feelings with your own words.

happy   sad   proud   embarrassed

calm   excited   angry   scared

I am feeling...

Date ....

Circle *FeelLinks* doll(s) that shows how you are feeling.

....

....

....

....

....

....

....

Now I am feeling...

Color *FeelLinks* doll(s) that shows how you are feeling now. Blank dolls can be used to label feelings with your own words.

happy   sad   proud   embarrassed

calm   excited   angry   scared

I am feeling...

Circle *FeelLinks* doll(s) that shows how you are feeling.

....

....

....

....

....

....

....

Now I am feeling...

Color *FeelLinks* doll(s) that shows how you are feeling now. Blank dolls can be used to label feelings with your own words.

| happy | sad | proud | embarrassed | |
| calm | excited | angry | scared | |

I am feeling...

Date ....

Circle *FeelLinks* doll(s) that shows how you are feeling.

....

....

....

....

....

....

....

Now I am feeling...

Color *FeelLinks* doll(s) that shows how you are feeling now. Blank dolls
can be used to label feelings with your own words.

happy   sad   proud   embarrassed

calm   excited   angry   scared

I am feeling...

Circle *FeelLinks* doll(s) that shows how you are feeling.

....

....

....

....

....

....

....

Now I am feeling...

Color *FeelLinks* doll(s) that shows how you are feeling now. Blank dolls can be used to label feelings with your own words.

| happy | sad | proud | embarrassed | |
| calm | excited | angry | scared | |

I am feeling...

Circle *FeelLinks* doll(s) that shows how you are feeling.

....

....

....

....

....

....

Now I am feeling...

Color *FeelLinks* doll(s) that shows how you are feeling now. Blank dolls can be used to label feelings with your own words.

happy   sad   proud   embarrassed

calm   excited   angry   scared

I am feeling...

Circle *FeelLinks* doll(s) that shows how you are feeling.

....

....

....

....

....

....

....

Now I am feeling...

Color *FeelLinks* doll(s) that shows how you are feeling now. Blank dolls can be used to label feelings with your own words.

happy   sad   proud   embarrassed

calm   excited   angry   scared

I am feeling...

Circle *FeelLinks* doll(s) that shows how you are feeling.

....
....
....
....
....
....
....

Now I am feeling...

Color *FeelLinks* doll(s) that shows how you are feeling now. Blank dolls can be used to label feelings with your own words.

happy   sad   proud   embarrassed

calm   excited   angry   scared

I am feeling...

Date ....

Circle *FeelLinks* doll(s) that shows how you are feeling.

....

....

....

....

....

....

....

Now I am feeling...

Color *FeelLinks* doll(s) that shows how you are feeling now. Blank dolls can be used to label feelings with your own words.

happy   sad   proud   embarrassed

calm   excited   angry   scared

I am feeling...

Circle *FeelLinks* doll(s) that shows how you are feeling.

....

....

....

....

....

....

....

Now I am feeling...

Color *FeelLinks* doll(s) that shows how you are feeling now. Blank dolls
can be used to label feelings with your own words.

happy   sad   proud   embarrassed

calm   excited   angry   scared

I am feeling...

Circle *FeelLinks* doll(s) that shows how you are feeling.

....

....

....

....

....

....

Now I am feeling...

Color *FeelLinks* doll(s) that shows how you are feeling now. Blank dolls can be used to label feelings with your own words.

happy   sad   proud   embarrassed

calm   excited   angry   scared

I am feeling...

Date................................

Circle *FeelLinks* doll(s) that shows how you are feeling.

....

....

....

....

....

....

....

Now I am feeling...

Color *FeelLinks* doll(s) that shows how you are feeling now. Blank dolls can be used to label feelings with your own words.

happy   sad   proud   embarrassed

calm   excited   angry   scared

I am feeling...

Date ....

Circle *FeelLinks* doll(s) that shows how you are feeling.

....

....

....

....

....

....

....

Now I am feeling...

Color *FeelLinks* doll(s) that shows how you are feeling now. Blank dolls can be used to label feelings with your own words.

| happy | sad | proud | embarrassed | |
| calm | excited | angry | scared | |

I am feeling...

Circle *FeelLinks* doll(s) that shows how you are feeling.

....

....

....

....

....

....

....

Now I am feeling...

Color *FeelLinks* doll(s) that shows how you are feeling now. Blank dolls can be used to label feelings with your own words.

happy   sad   proud   embarrassed

calm   excited   angry   scared

I am feeling...

Date ....

Circle *FeelLinks* doll(s) that shows how you are feeling.

....

....

....

....

....

....

....

Now I am feeling...

Color *FeelLinks* doll(s) that shows how you are feeling now. Blank dolls can be used to label feelings with your own words.

happy   sad   proud   embarrassed

calm   excited   angry   scared

I am feeling...

Date ....

Circle *FeelLinks* doll(s) that shows how you are feeling.

....

....

....

....

....

....

....

Now I am feeling...

Color *FeelLinks* doll(s) that shows how you are feeling now. Blank dolls
can be used to label feelings with your own words.

happy   sad   proud   embarrassed

calm   excited   angry   scared

I am feeling...

Date ....

Circle *FeelLinks* doll(s) that shows how you are feeling.

··

··

··

··

··

··

··

Now I am feeling...

Color *FeelLinks* doll(s) that shows how you are feeling now. Blank dolls can be used to label feelings with your own words.

| happy | sad | proud | embarrassed | |
| calm | excited | angry | scared | |

I am feeling...

Circle *FeelLinks* doll(s) that shows how you are feeling.

....

....

....

....

....

....

Now I am feeling...

Color *FeelLinks* doll(s) that shows how you are feeling now. Blank dolls can be used to label feelings with your own words.

happy   sad   proud   embarrassed

calm   excited   angry   scared

I am feeling...

Circle *FeelLinks* doll(s) that shows how you are feeling.

....

....

....

....

....

....

....

Now I am feeling...

Color *FeelLinks* doll(s) that shows how you are feeling now. Blank dolls can be used to label feelings with your own words.

| happy | sad | proud | embarrassed | |
| calm | excited | angry | scared | |

I am feeling...

Circle *FeelLinks* doll(s) that shows how you are feeling.

....

....

....

....

....

....

....

Now I am feeling...

Color *FeelLinks* doll(s) that shows how you are feeling now. Blank dolls can be used to label feelings with your own words.

happy   sad   proud   embarrassed

calm   excited   angry   scared

I am feeling...

Circle *FeelLinks* doll(s) that shows how you are feeling.

....

....

....

....

....

....

....

....

Now I am feeling...

Color *FeelLinks* doll(s) that shows how you are feeling now. Blank dolls can be used to label feelings with your own words.

happy   sad   proud   embarrassed

calm   excited   angry   scared

I am feeling...

Date ....

Circle *FeelLinks* doll(s) that shows how you are feeling.

....

....

....

....

....

....

....

Now I am feeling...

Color *FeelLinks* doll(s) that shows how you are feeling now. Blank dolls can be used to label feelings with your own words.

happy   sad   proud   embarrassed

calm   excited   angry   scared

I am feeling...

Circle *FeelLinks* doll(s) that shows how you are feeling.

....

....

....

....

....

....

....

Now I am feeling...

Color *FeelLinks* doll(s) that shows how you are feeling now. Blank dolls can be used to label feelings with your own words.

happy   sad   proud   embarrassed

calm   excited   angry   scared

I am feeling...

Date ....

Circle *FeelLinks* doll(s) that shows how you are feeling.

....

....

....

....

....

....

Now I am feeling...

Color *FeelLinks* doll(s) that shows how you are feeling now. Blank dolls
can be used to label feelings with your own words.

happy   sad   proud   embarrassed

calm   excited   angry   scared

I am feeling...

Date ....

Circle *FeelLinks* doll(s) that shows how you are feeling.

....

....

....

....

....

....

....

Now I am feeling...

Color *FeelLinks* doll(s) that shows how you are feeling now. Blank dolls can be used to label feelings with your own words.

| happy | sad | proud | embarrassed | |
| calm | excited | angry | scared | |

I am feeling...

Circle *FeelLinks* doll(s) that shows how you are feeling.

....

....

....

....

....

....

....

Now I am feeling...

Color *FeelLinks* doll(s) that shows how you are feeling now. Blank dolls can be used to label feelings with your own words.

happy   sad   proud   embarrassed

calm   excited   angry   scared

I am feeling...

Date ....

Circle *FeelLinks* doll(s) that shows how you are feeling.

....

....

....

....

....

....

Now I am feeling...

Color *FeelLinks* doll(s) that shows how you are feeling now. Blank dolls can be used to label feelings with your own words.

happy	sad	proud	embarrassed	
calm	excited	angry	scared	

I am feeling...

Circle *FeelLinks* doll(s) that shows how you are feeling.

....

....

....

....

....

....

....

Now I am feeling...

Color *FeelLinks* doll(s) that shows how you are feeling now. Blank dolls can be used to label feelings with your own words.

happy   sad   proud   embarrassed

calm   excited   angry   scared

I am feeling...

Date ....

Circle *FeelLinks* doll(s) that shows how you are feeling.

....

....

....

....

....

....

....

Now I am feeling...

Color *FeelLinks* doll(s) that shows how you are feeling now. Blank dolls can be used to label feelings with your own words.

happy   sad   proud   embarrassed

calm   excited   angry   scared

I am feeling...

Circle *FeelLinks* doll(s) that shows how you are feeling.

....

....

....

....

....

....

....

Now I am feeling...

Color *FeelLinks* doll(s) that shows how you are feeling now. Blank dolls can be used to label feelings with your own words.

happy   sad   proud   embarrassed

calm   excited   angry   scared

I am feeling...

Circle *FeelLinks* doll(s) that shows how you are feeling.

....

....

....

....

....

....

....

Now I am feeling...

Color *FeelLinks* doll(s) that shows how you are feeling now. Blank dolls can be used to label feelings with your own words.

happy   sad   proud   embarrassed

calm   excited   angry   scared

I am feeling...

Circle *FeelLinks* doll(s) that shows how you are feeling.

....

....

....

....

....

....

....

Now I am feeling...

Color *FeelLinks* doll(s) that shows how you are feeling now. Blank dolls can be used to label feelings with your own words.

happy   sad   proud   embarrassed

calm   excited   angry   scared

I am feeling...

Circle *FeelLinks* doll(s) that shows how you are feeling.

....

....

....

....

....

....

....

Now I am feeling...

Color *FeelLinks* doll(s) that shows how you are feeling now. Blank dolls
can be used to label feelings with your own words.

happy   sad   proud   embarrassed

calm   excited   angry   scared

I am feeling...

Date ....

Circle *FeelLinks* doll(s) that shows how you are feeling.

....

....

....

....

....

....

....

Now I am feeling...

Color *FeelLinks* doll(s) that shows how you are feeling now. Blank dolls
can be used to label feelings with your own words.

happy sad proud embarrassed

calm excited angry scared

I am feeling...

Circle *FeelLinks* doll(s) that shows how you are feeling.

....

....

....

....

....

....

....

Now I am feeling...

Color *FeelLinks* doll(s) that shows how you are feeling now. Blank dolls can be used to label feelings with your own words.

happy   sad   proud   embarrassed

calm   excited   angry   scared

I am feeling...

Circle *FeelLinks* doll(s) that shows how you are feeling.

....

....

....

....

....

....

Now I am feeling...

Color *FeelLinks* doll(s) that shows how you are feeling now. Blank dolls can be used to label feelings with your own words.

happy   sad   proud   embarrassed

calm   excited   angry   scared

I am feeling...

Circle *FeelLinks* doll(s) that shows how you are feeling.

....

....

....

....

....

....

....

Now I am feeling...

Color *FeelLinks* doll(s) that shows how you are feeling now. Blank dolls can be used to label feelings with your own words.

happy   sad   proud   embarrassed

calm   excited   angry   scared

Glossary

BASELINE – The state you return to after experiencing heightened emotions.

COMMUNICATION – The act or process of using words, sounds, signs, or behaviors to express or exchange information or to express your ideas, thoughts, feelings, etc. to someone else.

> **NON-VERBAL COMMUNICATION** – Behaviors such as facial and eye expressions, touching, tone of voice, and gestures or mannerisms, as well as dress, posture and spatial distance between two or more people.

> **VERBAL COMMUNICATION** – The use of sounds and words to express yourself, especially in contrast to using gestures or mannerisms (non-verbal communication).

EMOTION – Strong feeling, often accompanied by a physical reaction.

EMOTIONAL AWARENESS – Recognizing when you are feeling an emotion, the ability to identify your feelings, and being sensitive to the presence of emotions in others.

EMOTIONAL INTELLIGENCE – The capacity to be aware of, control, and express one's emotions, and to handle interpersonal relationships thoughtfully and empathetically.

EMOTIONAL LITERACY – One's ability to identify, understand and respond to emotions in themselves and others in a healthy manner.

EMOTIONAL VOCABULARY – One component of emotional literacy, which is necessary for children to regulate their emotions and engage in social interactions. Words like happy, sad, excited, scared are part of emotional vocabulary.

FEELING – An emotional state or reaction.

SELF-AWARENESS – One's ability to accurately recognize and name their own thoughts and emotions and how they influence behaviors.

SELF-MANAGEMENT – One's ability to effectively regulate emotions, behaviors and thoughts during various situations.

SOCIAL AWARENESS – One's ability to empathize and take the perspective of others. Interact in a proper manner.

REGULATE – The ability of an individual to control one emotion or set of emotions. Emotion regulation requires conscious monitoring and using techniques in order to manage situations better.

> **CO-REGULATION** – A warm and responsive interaction when an adult provides support, coaching and modeling children need to understand, express and reduce the intensity of emotions.

RELATIONSHIP SKILLS – Establishing and maintaining healthy relationships with different groups and individuals. This includes communicating, listening, cooperating, resisting social pressure, problem-solving, and seeking and offering help to others.

Feeling Definitions

ANGRY – Strongly feeling great annoyance, pain, trouble or displeasure.
ANNOYED – Being made angry by someone or something.
CRANKY – Being easily angered.
ENVIOUS – Resentful, usually because you want something that someone else has.
FRUSTRATED – Feeling you did not get what you want or need.
FUMING – So angry, like steam is coming out of your ears.
FURIOUS – Extremely angry.
GRUMPY – In a bad mood.
IRRITATED – Feeling displeasured or stirred to anger.
JEALOUS – Feeling envy of what someone else has or can do. Resentful.
MAD – Very displeased.
OVERWHELMED – Overcome with emotion.
STRESSED – Feeling mental or emotional strain or tension.
UPSET – Worried, angered or unhappy.

CALM – Free from excitement or disturbance.
CONTENT – Satisfied.
FULFILLED – Having everything you need.
PEACEFUL – Enjoying peace and quiet.
RELAXED – Not worried or tense.
RELIEVED – Without fear or worry.
RESTFUL – Relax, sleep or without activity.
SATISFIED – Happy with what you have; needing nothing else.
TRANQUIL – Without noise or excitement.

EMBARRASSED – Feeling self-consciously confused or distressed.
ASHAMED – Feeling shame or guilt.
AWKWARD – Causing embarrassment. Lacking in skill.
CONFUSED – Unable to understand or think clearly.
FLUSTERED – Nervous confusion.
SELF-CONSCIOUS – Being aware of yourself and questioning how you appear to others.
SHY – Not feeling comfortable around others; not wanting or being able to call attention to yourself.
UNCOMFORTABLE – Uneasy feeling in your body.

EXCITED – Having or showing a strong energized feeling.
EAGER – Having or showing an impatient or enthusiastic interest or desire.
ECSTATIC – Overwhelming, extreme pleasurable emotion.
ENTHUSIASTIC – Liking something a lot and being very interested in it.
THRILLED – Experiencing a sudden, strong feeling of excitement.

HAPPY – Feeling great pleasure or joy.
CHEERFUL – Bright and pleasant.
FORTUNATE – Having good luck.
FULFILLED – Happy and satisfied about life.
GLAD – Experiencing pleasure, joy or delight.
GLOWING- So happy and satisfied that you feel like you are glowing.
GRATEFUL – The quality of feeling thankful.
JOYFUL – Full of joy, very happy.
MERRY – Smiling and cheerful.
THANKFUL – Feeling or showing of appreciation.

PROUD – Displaying excessive self-esteem and self-respect.
BRAVE – Feeling or displaying no fear; courageous.
CONFIDENT – Self-assured in your own powers and abilities.
COURAGEOUS – Not letting fear hold you back. Doing what is right.
DELIGHTED – Extremely happy.
FULFILLED - Feeling that your abilities and talents are fully being used.

SAD – Filled with grief or unhappiness.
DISAPPOINTED – Upset over something that is not like you thought it would be.
GLOOMY – Everything feels darker than usual; causing feelings of sadness.
GRIEF – Deep sadness; especially for the loss of someone or something.
GRUMPY – In a bad, sad mood.
HEARTBROKEN – Extremely sad, like your heart is breaking into pieces.
HELPLESS – Feeling there is no one to help you.
HURT – Unhappiness or sadness caused by someone's words or actions.
LONELY – Being alone and feeling sad about it.
MOPEY – Droopy and sad.
UNHAPPY – Not cheerful.
UPSET – Unhappy like you could cry.

SCARED – Being in a state of fear, fright or panic.
AFRAID – Filled with concern or fear.
ANXIOUS – Worried something is going to happen that will be scary for you.
CONCERNED – Worried or anxious about a person or thing.
FEARFUL – Full of fear or worry about danger.
JITTERY – Jumpy with nerves.
NERVOUS – Edgy, worried and jumpy.
PANICKED – Out of control with fear.
SHOCKED – Stunned, dazed and upset.
STRESSED – Worried and frazzled.
TENSE – Your muscles have tensed up, your jaw is clenched, and you are worried.
TERRIFIED – Scared stiff.
WORRIED – Concerned and anxious about something.

References

Brackett, Marc. Yale Center for Emotional Intelligence. www.ycei.org. www.rulerapproach.org.

Brackett, Marc. (2019). *Permission to Feel*. New York: Celadon Books, 2019. Print.

Center on the Developing Child, Harvard University.

Center on the Social and Emotional Foundations for Early Learning http://csefel.vanderbilt.edu/index.html.

Collaborative for Academic, Social, and Emotional Learning. Casel.org.

Committee for Children – Secondstep.org.

Goleman, Daniel. (1995). *Emotional Intelligence*. New York: Bantam Books, 1995. Print.

Gottman Institute. www.gottman.com.

Mayer, J.D., & Salovey, P. (1997).

Social and Emotional Learning Framework

According to the Collaborative for Academic, Social, and Emotional Learning (CASEL, 2017), the social and emotional learning process can be achieved with the following framework. *FeelLinks* was developed taking each of these important components into consideration:

Self-Awareness

The ability to accurately recognize one's own emotions, thoughts, and values and how they influence behavior. The ability to accurately assess one's strengths and limitations, with a well-grounded sense of confidence, optimism, and a "growth mindset."

Social Awareness

The ability to take the perspective of and empathize with others, including those from diverse backgrounds and cultures. The ability to understand social and ethical norms for behavior and to recognize family, school, and community resources and supports.

Responsible Decision-Making

The ability to make constructive choices about personal behavior and social interactions based on ethical standards, safety concerns, and social norms. The realistic evaluation of consequences of various actions, and a consideration of the well-being of oneself and others.

Self-Management

The ability to successfully regulate one's emotions, thoughts, and behaviors in different situations — effectively managing stress, controlling impulses, and motivating oneself. The ability to set and work toward personal and academic goals.

Relationship Skills

The ability to establish and maintain healthy and rewarding relationships with diverse individuals and groups. The ability to communicate clearly, listen well, cooperate with others, resist inappropriate social pressure, negotiate conflict constructively, and seek and offer help when needed.

This framework is a product of the Collaborative for Academic, Social, and Emotional Learning (©2017 CASEL) and is available at casel.org.